A grateful heart

is the friend of happiness,

inner peace, and joy.

Gratitude reveals

love's presence

face to face.

To accept the wonder of love

with gratitude

is to amplify that power

until you feel

its currents and surges

as the lifeblood flowing

through your veins.

Salute the dawn,

the rising sun of your

higher consciousness,

with gratitude

for the flame of life

within your beating heart.

Be grateful for everything—

the stars, the sun,

your family and friends,

your nation, and the world.

Gratitude increases

the ability of your heart

to attract the good.

Kindness is a flower

in the garden of gratitude.

With gratitude welling up
continually in your heart,
you cannot help but share
what you have with others.

Show gratitude to others

by acknowledging

the good that they do.

Uplift them and open the door

through which they can step

into their higher potential.

Express gratitude

even for small accomplishments,

for some little task

done well by another.

Feelings of gratitude

heighten your sensitivity

to the inner voice

and enhance your connection.

Gratitude goes hand in hand
with a refined appreciation
of life, art, and beauty.
Gratitude is a means of fine-tuning
the senses of your soul.

Through the lens of gratitude,

you more easily perceive

the richness of life

all around you.

Gratitude sees the divine

within the commonplace.

Gratitude is a mighty

torrent of love.

It opens the floodgates

of the heart and melts

the frozen waters of the mind.

Gratitude moves along the higher

cadences of mankind's tender

and compassionate feelings

toward one another.

Gratitude is a fountain

that flows out of love,

and by gratitude

you start love flowing.

Become like a flower—

fragrant with purpose

and manifesting a sense

of divine appreciation.

Morning's
Dew

Start counting your blessings
when you awake in the morning
and expand that feeling
throughout the day.
Go to sleep with a prayer
of gratitude in your heart.

Light rays of gratitude

reach the heart of God,

and in response

the Father's blessing

flows into your world.

Through a flowing
stream of gratitude,
joy can fill your heart
and bubble over.

If gratitude does not
come easily to you,
practice daily in private
to reflect on the good things
you now have in your life.
As surely as you
keep up this practice,
more reasons to be grateful
will come to you.

Make a list of things
that bring you joy.
Start with just one thing
and then keep going.

Affirming your gratitude
is a wondrous way
to continually perceive
the joy flame of life.

When you enjoy something
for its beauty or function,
you treat it with care.
In this way you honor
and show your appreciation
for the gift and the giver.
This is gratitude.

Offering gratitude

for things small and great

prepares you for the next steps

of a wondrous transformation.

Let feelings of joy,

appreciation, and gratitude

play upon the harp

of your heart.

Beauty and loveliness

are easily perceived in nature,

especially in flowers.

To cultivate appreciation

and gratitude,

begin with flowers.

Then expand your awareness

until you can perceive

the perfume of a soul

as you would a rose.

Write a short note to someone,

expressing your gratitude

for who they are,

the role they play in your life,

and what you have learned

from them.

Pray with gratitude

and with all the love

of your heart.

Bring all the resources

of your being

to your prayer.

Then you will see

tremendous change

in your life.

Many offer thanks

for food, substance, and shelter,

for sea, earth, and sky.

Be one who also gives thanks

for life and illumination,

for the ideals, qualities,

and inspirations that manifest

within you and in your life.

Recognize the power of gratitude.
Expansive feelings of gratitude
bring buoyancy to your life
and work wonders in your body
as well as in your mind.

Especially on your birthday,

express your joy and gratitude

for the gift of life.

In that state of gratitude,

offer a prayer from your heart

for all life on earth.

When gratitude

pours forth from your heart

in great waves of love,

there is always a return current,

a release of energy

that returns a blessing to you.

You appreciate someone
because you understand them,
you see the beauty within them,
you see who they really are.

Gratitude is an appreciation
of all that is lovely
about a person.

Most people do not appreciate

all that they ought to

about themselves.

They take themselves for granted.

By acknowledging the qualities
you appreciate in others,
you help them to focus
their appreciation inward.
This can assist them to hear
the still, small voice speaking
words of sweet love to them.

A child's offering

is always pure;

hence, it is always beautiful.

When you show gratitude

for a child's offering,

you give that child

a lifelong memory

of having brought you a gift

that you received

with gratitude and happiness,

a memory of feeling

your appreciation of them

and what they did.

Become as a little child

in the wonder of life!

See how grateful you become

for little things

and how unattached

to the accumulation of objects,

wealth, stature, or greatness

in the eyes of the world.

Your gratitude for every gift

that life has given you

cascades from your heart

in concentric waves of light

and returns again to you.

As you give,

so shall you receive.

A Grassy Spot

Gratitude is the herald

of buoyant joy.

For joy to flower,

it must be planted

in the soil of gratitude.

Appreciation and gratitude

establish your connection

with the Giver of All Gifts.

By offering gratitude

for what you have,

you create an opening

through which more can flow

into your life.

Gratitude opens the door

to abundance.

When you start counting

your blessings,

you will find so many

that you can afford

to give generously

and still have plenty.

Let gratitude flow

into all the problem areas

of your life.

You will be amazed

at how much control

you have over yourself

and your situation.

Whatever your current

circumstances, possessions,

virtues, and self-awareness—

the more gratitude you feel

for what you have right now,

the more you will find fulfillment.

No matter what befalls you,

you can be grateful for it,

for there will always be

a hidden blessing in it

or something to be learned.

Challenges teach lessons

and responsibility.

They force you to sharpen

the tools of your mind,

heart, soul, and body.

Being grateful for challenges

is a key to your victory.

Gratitude flows

when you learn

from your mistakes

and recognize your opportunity

to move forward

and transcend yourself.

Self-analysis

of your performance

can help you to improve,

especially when you

also give gratitude

for what you have

already accomplished.

Be grateful for adversity

and for enemies.

Self-mastery comes

from working through

flaws and problems.

Wrongs done to you

give you an opportunity

to learn forgiveness, to grow,

and to be more the master

of your life.

From this perspective,

you can be grateful for everyone

that has ever wronged you

and for every life experience.

When you are able

to forgive and let go,

when you can have mercy

for those who have caused harm,

when you can feel grateful

for tough lessons learned—

then you can be healed,

you can become whole.

To overcome an aversion,

cultivate gratitude

for who or what a person is.

Find something to like

about that one

and you will find it

impossible to feel dislike.

The great love tide

of appreciation

softens all discord,

enabling you to embrace

the overcoming spirit of life.

Show gratitude

for forgiveness and mercy

in your life

by being forgiving

and merciful

toward others.

Forgiveness

is the handmaid

of gratitude.

Gratitude

is an effective antidote

for anger, anxiety,

sadness, and depression.

If you feel sad or worried,

remind yourself of all

that you are thankful for.

Forget about what you lack.

Worry, doubt, and fear attract

exactly what you don't want.

Keep your mind on gratitude

for the good that you have

and the good that you

desire to attract.

The recipe for mastering feelings

is to live in a perpetual

state of gratitude.

Make a habit of feeling

intensely grateful

to be alive and well,

and see how quickly

your problems will be solved.

In the very moment

that you begin

to express gratitude

for the design of perfection

for your life,

you begin the release

of that perfection

into your world.

Each time you serve life,

you contact the heart of creation

and receive in return

a flow of gratitude as a spark,

a transfer of energy.

Gratitude for life

sustains spiritual nourishment.

As you develop

an ever-greater sense

of gratitude,

you will radiate joy,

a sense of peace, comfort,

and healing to life.

CLIMBING IVY

As you bless with gratitude

who you are

and what you have

in this moment,

you expand it.

The power of multiplication

is within your consciousness.

Let go the memory of mistakes

except insofar as

not to repeat them.

Hold in your awareness

kindnesses done for you,

for these will fill your mind

with love and gratitude.

Besides counting

how far you must go

before you arrive at a goal,

take time to affirm

and express your gratitude

for progress already made.

Be profoundly grateful
for gifts and graces,
and never take them
for granted.

If you are tempted
to have doubt or fear,
tapping into the spirit
of gratitude and appreciation
can shift your state of mind.

Give gratitude to your body

for allowing you to do

the work you do,

to live the life you lead.

Love your body.

Care for it as you would

care for your child.

Pulsating life flows

continually into your body.

Send back gratitude

from your heart

for the gift of life.

When you see

something wonderful,

express gratitude for it

without looking for anything

that might be wrong with it.

Gratitude sustains the flow

of grace, light, and life!

Let your expressions

of gratitude

carry the light of your heart.

Gratitude releases

the love fires of the heart.

Bear difficulties gracefully,

honorably, and with gratitude

even as you forgive others

and ask for forgiveness.

Allow yourself to go forth

free and renewed.

Travails and difficulties

are like a rough winter.

If you appreciate them

and master them,

you will come out stronger

for having passed through them,

and you will appreciate

the summer a little bit more.

Greet all of life's

experiences and trials

as opportunities

to express gratitude

and to continue to love.

In gratitude,

give of yourself

and see how you become

more refined,

more of your real self.

The gratitude that parents

and teachers show for children

plays an important role

in instilling in them

a sense of self-worth

and self-acceptance.

Appreciation of children

helps them

to appreciate themselves.

Instead of always finding
something to correct in children,
form a habit of appreciating
and accepting them
for who and what they are.

Go out of your way
to acknowledge
and appreciate others.
Thank them for their
contribution,
whether good work
or a sunny disposition.
The more you reinforce positives,
the more often you will
see them repeated.

Let your heart be quickened
with immense joy and gratitude
for the little things people do,
for the sunbeam coming
through your window,
for loving friends and family.

When you walk in the hills,

be thankful for nature

in all her glory—

the mountains and clouds,

the grasses in a million varieties,

the wonders of the wildflowers,

the beauty that surrounds you.

Give thanks for

the wonderful things of life

that are so often

taken for granted.

Reflecting on the reasons
you are grateful for someone
will help you remember
to appreciate them more.

Sit quietly sometime
and reflect on the people
for whom you are grateful.
You will see positive changes
in your thoughts and attitude.

Before the sun sets on your day,

share your troubles in prayer

and say “thank you”

for all the good things

that happened that day.

Thereby God knows

that you are grateful

and also knows

what you need to resolve.

Be grateful

for lessons learned,

wisdom gained,

and the people you have met

along the way.

Feel gratitude

for the light

in which you bask—

the light that supports

all life.

Your expressions of gratitude
send forth a radiance
of positive energy
that benefits all life.

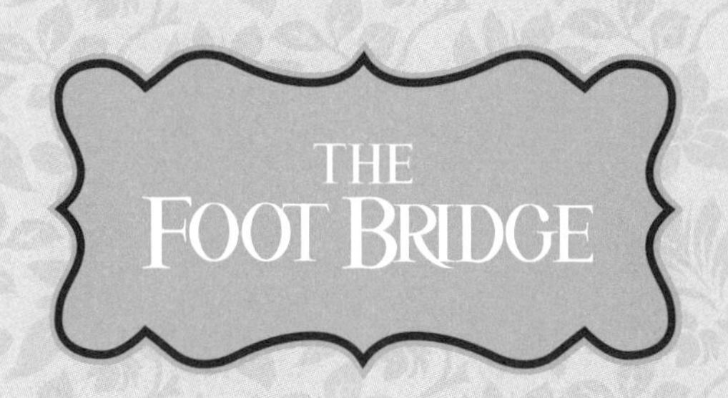

THE FOOT BRIDGE

Gratitude enters the heart

as a gentle radiance,

releasing the power of spirit

into the world

in a physical way.

Appreciation enhances

the value of all that life

has bestowed.

As you develop gratitude,

you dwell even more

in those gifts and graces.

Acknowledging your gratitude

and feeling it deeply

anchors what you receive,

allowing you

to become one with it

through joy.

A smile is the sign

of a grateful heart.

Gratitude in your heart

bursts over the very

boundaries of your consciousness

and floods the whole world.

The flood of gratitude

affects every condition,

and all life becomes more real.

On the waves of your gratitude,

heaven releases to you

the fountainhead of love,

creativity, and inspiration.

The transcendent beauty
that infuses enduring
concepts, works of art,
and other lasting creations
has been brought forth
through the gratitude
of the receptive heart.

The welling up of gratitude
can transform your life
into a sublime expression
of gratitude and abundance.

Miracles occur in the lives

of those who are grateful—

for out of gratitude are spun

a sense and a space

for more grace to come.

Sustained feelings of gratitude

rise like a pathway of light.

They soar beyond the stars

and return to your grateful heart

the energy to maintain

an inner balance

despite outer conditions.

At sunset,

pause for a moment,

stand and face the sun

as it disappears

from the horizon,

and feel intense gratitude

for a glorious day.

The mystery of giving thanks

is that gratitude for the good

multiplies the good.

When you live

in a state of gratitude,

you tap into a power

that can help shape the future

for the collective good

of all humanity.

Lavishly has the Creator

bestowed upon you

his kingdom.

With gratitude,

lavishly receive it.

Let the gratitude

of your heart

be boundless.

Gardens of the Heart Series

Compassion

Gratitude

Forgiveness

Joy

Jardines del corazón

Compasión

Gratitud

Perdón

Alegría

For other titles by
Elizabeth Clare Prophet,
please visit

www.SummitUniversityPress.com